Business opportunities for times of crisis

Important business opportunities are emerging in the world, all thanks to a wide variety of sectors that are currently booming, so you need to know how you can take advantage of the business ideas with the greatest potential to change your life.

By knowing the topic that is generating the best economic results, you will be able to dedicate attention and effort to carry out these ideas, so that you can be part of the global entrepreneurship that can be developed in the digital environment, where there are many alternatives to invest freely.

How to undertake and take advantage of business opportunities

Taking advantage of business opportunities is within everyone's reach, but the ease or level of success is not the same for each entrepreneur, so to better face this path, it is vital to take into account different factors, this implies that each phase of a business is a starting point to be estimated.

The phases of entrepreneurship can be adapted to any business idea, so that it is not imposed as a rigid model, but can

be customized to the techniques of analysis of results that provide greater success, considering the following phases:

- **SWOT Analysis**

The materialization of the SWOT analysis, at first glance may seem very basic, but it is worth considering one by one the weaknesses, strengths, threats and opportunities facing a business, being a broader point of view to work for an improvement, by making a table with these four points, you can take note of each aspect.

This process of evaluating a business can be carried out in a very short period of time, allowing you to learn more about the project, the team and the demands of the sector, providing an accurate picture of the context or the situation that the business must face.

- **Choose a business idea you are passionate about and have a market for**

A business idea requires perseverance, so it is vital to choose a path that can awaken passion, so that this dedication of time is not seen as torture, it is mostly based on doing or paying attention to what you like, and to this issue, we add the

equation of having a potential audience, to make it a profitable business.

As long as it is a type of business with enough customers, you can choose to generate a significant flow of sales, reaching the point of defining a niche that allows you to carry out a pleasant commercial action, you just have to have a viable market share.

- **Choose a business idea**

Once you have the desire to start a business, the next thing to do is to dedicate time to measuring the business idea, it is a key point that must be passed through the previous points to measure its success, so you can continue in the establishment of an attractive business, maintaining a powerful mindset.

The best trick to choose an effective business idea, is that it is a solution or answer to some need, this helps to detect a wide margin of profitability, because any complaint or unattended requirement can be monetized, that helps every venture to obtain a positive scale pro analyzing market complaints.

In the midst of this decision about the business idea, you can think of a topic that is working in another location, in addition to having some kind of thematic monitoring, in addition to reading trends that help to follow the line of attraction, and any other form of measurement.

- **Validation of the business idea**

Once a business idea has been identified, the next thing to do is to validate it, this is a study prior to the business venture, on the other hand you can implement tools that can be applied to publicize the business in style, to measure the impact of the theme of a business.

- **Differential means of competition**

Behind every business idea, there is a level of competition behind, for that reason, it is a must to make sure to bring something new that is of value, also if it is a busy sector is because it generates profits, from a unique approach, so that instead of fighting with the competition, you can stand out with your virtues.

- **Specialization**

All kinds of entrepreneurship require specialization, so that a much more concrete offering can be created, for this it is essential to awaken its multitasking approach, seeking to stand out from the competition, and leaving aside that generic classification, that helps to connect with a greater number of customers.

The growth in this commercial field depends directly on the presentation as an expert that can be made, and with higher certification, higher charges can be incorporated.

- **Establishing the buyer persona**

The fictitious representation of a client is of great help to focus completely on the needs coverage, it is much easier to postulate yourself as interesting to the target audience, when you know them in depth, this type of discovery of qualities is highly useful.

Tips for developing a business opportunity

Nowadays, in order to stand out and progress, it is necessary to inquire about the ideas with the greatest opportunity, the trends that can serve as inspiration to form a business, and even the projects that have the greatest boom in order to reach the expected level of development.

Once this type of research or discovery is carried out, it is only necessary to study how it can be applied and conquer the chosen market, for this it is vital to analyze each business model, so that a successful example can be replicated effectively, for each business activity, it is only necessary to adapt.

Before launching any business idea, you need to implement the following tips as an effective realization:

- **Geographical adaptation**

An initial point to underline is that a business opportunity can generate a boom in certain geographic locations, but this does not mean that when implemented in other geographic areas it will have the same potential for success, for this reason, it is necessary to investigate the obstacles of that sector and study the feasibility of the idea.

- **Get to know the business model**

A simple business idea does not come to life unless you study in greater detail what that business model represents, because this is the way in which you can discover some part that can be adapted to that environment, or that allows you to design a strategy so that the development of that idea can be profitable.

- **Choose what you are passionate about**

Faced with so much business diversity, a correct method of choice is to review your personal background and passion, so that it is a clear orientation on a business opportunity, using the most of your experience in that sector, so you can devote a greater amount of time without feeling bored, but more passion.

- **The financial factor is a variable**

The development of a business opportunity also depends on the proportion of budget needed for that purpose, so it is important to take into account the type of resources required for that specific business model, which helps to find the investments that work as a commercial impulse.

- **Analyzes the market and competition**

Every business opportunity must be estimated based on the existing level of competition, especially in the place where it will be developed, in addition to the way other similar businesses operate, can be used as an example itself, it is an improved and real vision of where you are looking to get to.

- **Member consideration**

To be part of certain markets, it is vital to have some partners to have a greater participation, because some business models need to have more support during the launch and positioning, it is essential to seek to go far with allies, than to go alone in some venture and decay.

Each one of these tips are analysis estimates, so that a business opportunity can be implemented with greater productivity, since each idea can be innovative and with a wide economic power, but if it is not applied in a proper and well thought out way, it will not generate the expected results.

Software-based productive business trends

The modern market has important trends, they represent a full boom due to the level of profits and benefits they generate for people, for that reason they are becoming an alternative that you should take into account, to think of a venture related to this trend or incorporate it into any business.

1. **Applying Big Data for crowdfunding success**

Every crowdfunding campaign that seeks to achieve its objectives relies entirely on big data, although this sector is still in full research for entrepreneurs, but this is a key alternative for

business campaigns to obtain a large margin of success, until they reach planned commercial results.

The development of a crowdfunding campaign can be reflected or made a reality through platforms that facilitate this task by means of big data, as it is a system through which data is analyzed in real time, being useful for the organization of a campaign to be effective.

Online is a plethora of crowdfunding options, to extend a $500,000 grant, so that anyone can have a commercial launch, and thus can reach a wide scale commercial idea, opportunities abound today.

2. The world of applications

The dedication or incursion into the world of applications, one of the most common aspects or needs, is that each application is sought to get out of that zombie life or function, that kind of inactivity needs to be corrected in time, especially because it is a lack of foresight on the part of its designer.

This kind of situation can make the development task or goal complex, as well as the type of marketing that can be done

on an application, even monetization, these aspects are controlled with Appurify solutions so that developers have the opportunity to have a remote test.

Through the cloud, native applications, web applications, and even on iOS and Android devices, on the other hand, there is also the function of Google Ventures, within this class of software arises Testim, being an option that uses artificial intelligence to ensure the creation, execution, maintenance and performance testing.

This kind of studies, helps the application to pass reliability parameters, and also facilitates its classification, so knowing and using these softwares is a profitable measure, another option is Wisebatt being a very useful platform to carry out the simulations and is loved by electronic engineers.

The design of devices, as well as IoT issues, so these solutions facilitate the operation on some hadware, all these efforts are known as virtual design or creation, and may require a great deal of investment and prototyping.

3. The podcast market

One of the trending markets with an underrated ranking is that of podcasts, but before opting for that space, you have

to know how to make each launch profitable, thus becoming a safe bet, to reach that point you can think of two projects or formulas.

One of the projects to exploit the podcast sector is Spreaker, a platform created in New York, which has a wide variety of functions that allow the creation, dissemination and monetization of podcast creations, and on the other hand there is Acast, defined as a Swedish platform for free use.

With the use of Acast, each user can discover and even share content, therefore, it is an opportunity for creators to find a great result that will boost their popularity, without forgetting the publication or broadcast of other types of content in addition to audio, such as encales and images.

4. **Commercialization of waste**

The action of reusing products has become a distinguished trend, for that reason it is a profitable business when a large proportion of success is invested, to reach that point it is vital to research and adopt more knowledge about that area, as well as to seek the support of some expert.

In the waste environment, two model projects stand out, firstly Comet Biorefining is a Canadian idea where technology is incorporated into the conversion of waste into glucose syrup, this is a recycling that provides an ample source of sugar.

Another interesting measure is that of CelluComp, although its dynamics is just the opposite of the previous mentioned, is a Scottish company that seeks to market sustainable products, from some waste streams that are part of the food industry, that type of waste is converted into manufacturing of household items.

5. **The change to a much healthier plastic**

Over time, the damage caused by plastic has placed it as a harmful element for the environment, and this classification has generated a wide option for entrepreneurship with innovative launches, such as edible straws, and a wide list of biodegradable products.

Auara is an opportunity to finance projects of this nature, since it is a company dedicated to the sale of bottles with 100% recycled plastic, and for this reason I support similar initiatives.

An additional alternative is the Dutch company Avantium, where an important dedication to the commercialization of plastics, together with chemical products, establishes this kind of consideration to innovate with plant-based plastics, a new generation of investment.

6. Utilities against blackouts

The loss of money due to blackouts is a clear problem for a great diversity of companies. In the face of these problems, several companies such as Dispatchr, through which alternatives are provided to cover the incidents with the electrical networks, and study the reduction of the duration of the electrical outages.

For this reason, the design of software to detect any failure on electrical networks, is a preventive aid of great level so that the risks can be reduced considerably, it is a technological analysis that leaves aside the problems in the face of blackouts, to this is added the help of artificial intelligence as an energy aid.

7. Smart cars and smart cities

In the market, the aspects of the future are valued in great detail, and one of the elements that are being much more

affected by this evolution are vehicles and cities, because more and more efficient tools are being incorporated into daily life, and in the midst of this community, a great deal of information on the subject is circulating.

This is a very large market, which is why there are platforms such as Motorq, where mobile data is managed to share data about cars, and Applied Intuition, which is a dedication to vehicle companies seeking to develop software.

8. Medical device incubator

The launch of a new product in any market is not a safe action, for this reason the health market is looking for alternatives that contribute to a much more measured development, this is the case of Inceptus Medical, a means through which engineers can manage the devices in advance.

Predictive marketing also plays a key role in these medical advances, for this purpose DocCheer can be used, as it is considered an aid for devices to follow a much more personalized line for customers, for that reason every new medical device is a quest for satisfaction.

Every market, every aspect of daily life has business trends, especially with the momentum of technology, that kind of power helps more opportunities arise, both innovation and self-improvement, as long as there is attachment to the software, these and more measures are a point of growth for any entrepreneur.

What you should know about crowdfunding

When it comes to entrepreneurship, the crowdfunding action should be taken into account, as it is a way to raise funds to commercially boost a business, but carrying out a campaign of this type requires knowledge to take advantage of the opportunities of the platforms available for this activity.

Basically this is a technique that brings together a large number of investors, but as it is not a traditional model, it is a lower concentration of investors, in addition to options where access to loans is generated, but to reach that level an ideal strategy must be developed that emits the idea on the public.

The way to prove the potential of a product is by launching it on that observation of investors, it is a way for the business to finish exploding in a feasible way, you just have to promote that business idea, looking for each project to shine by its own strengths until monetizing that admiration.

The basic actions of crowdfunding are developed through fundraising activities, on the other hand you can also launch a crowdfunding campaign, so that for a period of time you get that level of funding, and then run a completion behavior, where the funds received are returned.

The types of crowdfunding campaign, have to do with a participation where shares are shared, in exchange for the capital of the business, secondly donations arise, being a receipt of the fund without condition, and then there is the reward mode to overcome different levels to reach that figure cap sought.

The advantages of this line of progress or obtaining funding, is to measure the potential of an idea, audience formation or community that has empathy with your business, and is an easy access to have funding on your idea or project.

Find out how to determine the level of financing for a business

The presentation of a business idea to take advantage of an opportunity, must have an economic study, because it helps to determine the amount needed for the commercial launch, but many are the doubts about this study, for that, the business initiative must go through the following process:

- **Staff**

The number of personnel to be hired is an important variable, for this reason it is essential to question how many people are needed for the development of the business, and then measure the type of remuneration that this entails.

- **Development**

The scalability of a business can be estimated by means of the type of financial resources that are necessary, especially for the acquisition of tools that allow a business idea to function, as a consideration of the ingredients that need to be played.

- **Advertising**

Every business must think about the right way to make itself known, at this point is where advertising fits in, it is a useful investment nowadays, as well as the lines of communication with the customer.

Each of these factors should not be overlooked in an economic estimate of a business, so to know how much financing is required for the business to get started, this map or timeline

of a business idea is useful so that the figures can speak for themselves.

How to finance the commercial launch of a project

The disadvantages to have your own business, have much to do with the economic aspect, most advised to opt for bank loans, aid to government agencies, or think of business incubators, to think of partnerships or sponsorships, ie there are many ways to raise funds for projects.

But before getting to that point, the most important thing is to have a business idea, as it is the main seed for a project to come to fruition, the rest is translated into the necessary resources so that it can transcend, for each business topic you can think of a way of financing.

Many smaller projects can take their first steps in the commercial sector by means of microcredits, on the other hand, the Smart capital route has been implemented as a solution, or the aids that are provided by public agencies, beyond this choice, the essential thing is that it combines with the type of market.

In order to choose the financing method that best suits the business, the desired amount, the repayment term, as well as the assumable risk must be studied, so that the type of loan that is most useful for the business can be considered, as well as the type of collateral required to have access to it.

But in the midst of these decisions, it is important to consider the issue of debt, since depending on the level or magnitude of the debt, the participation of investors can be considered, although this type of capital also implies sharing future profits, although the contribution of knowledge and experience, which is of enormous value, must be taken into account.

Today's financing instruments are diverse, each one can be studied in comparison of pros and cons:

1. Bootstraping

It means in its literary translation; to put on the boot, which alludes to setting up a business without external help, seeking to use one's own savings as a defense, to then reduce expenses as much as possible, this implies making investments that are controlled, but in each movement it is crucial to capture information.

Depending on how the first investments of the product turn out, future decisions can be made, thus scaling up to the first revenues under a thorough sales tactic.

2. **Family and friends**

A viable alternative for a business to take off, is to bet on the FFF mode, these figures are adapted to the meaning of family, fools and friends, being an access to large amounts, this is a fast way and without so many requirements because it is not a bank, far from it.

The repayment time can also be negotiated, and the issue of interest as well, in some cases these funds are obtained for free, they are funds that become a kind of donation, this was the path followed by Jeff Bezos to establish Amazon, using that family impulse to create an effective business plan.

3. **Bank loan**

The banking sector is available to cover feasible business ideas, therefore they have financial instruments such as microcredits, loans dedicated to entrepreneurs, and even credits with special conditions, which are related to a business for social purpose.

Although this kind of avenues, requires a line of mediation and presentation of viable data, beyond these estimates, each applicant faces interest rates ranging from 3.5% to 7.5% per annum, but the advantage is that this allows you to remain in control of 100% of the business capital.

Popular entities in the world like Caixa, where it is possible to have access to loans that have a high value for the support of the modern entrepreneur, where the only requirement is to present a business plan that can demonstrate the viability, without forgetting any kind of assumptions, and with clarity about income as well as expenses.

4. **Public subsidies**

In the midst of building a strong business, another option that often works is the help of public agencies, this can be through grants as well as soft loans, this kind of entities are imposed at the continental level, so that more businesses can be created as long as they demonstrate their scalable role.

In order to have this type of aid, it is vital that the project complies with social and environmental purposes, as this causes the business to be valued from other perspectives, although another requirement is that they are not the only means of

financing, so if you meet these qualities, it is possible to have this access.

5. Incubators and accelerators

Currently there are a variety of platforms for incubation and acceleration of building a business, where both provide the advantage of having access to a variety of training, being a great help for entrepreneurship, and with the advantage of gaining capital for a business.

The essential thing is to think about the training or exchange that can provide greater value, for that level it is necessary to have the requirement of having experience, in addition to a good reputation, so that it is easier for the contacts to be focused on developing that business idea.

6. Crowdfunding

When it comes to obtaining funds, this measure is a help to have access to an important variety of small investors, it all depends on the type of platform you can choose, as well as the potentiality that is part of the business, that way you can gain a kind of disinterested investment.

On the other hand, it is also possible to generate an investment in exchange for equity participation, or loans under an interest threshold, it is a way to reach fast funding, being useful for all kinds of entrepreneurs, and most of these platforms have legal regulation.

7. Business angels and financing rounds

Once the business has interesting metrics that support its scaling, you can present these developments as a round to attract funding, so that investors have access to that commercial offering you provide, you can also opt for business angels known as venture capital funds.

This type of investment is not only in charge of providing money, but also experts in that sector that can provide knowledge, as well as their connections in the industry. It is a form of investment in line and not in points, because they are looking for a direct relationship with the business that can be sustained over time.

Many entrepreneurs and millionaires have made their dreams come true through these channels, so if you do not have liquidity at the beginning of the business, you can bet on additional support, it is also a litmus test to measure the feasibility of a business idea.

Business ideas for each productive sector

Setting up a business requires a high dose of inspiration, so you can take advantage of this opportunity to form a successful business, for this reason, know more business ideas in the sectors of great need, which are divided through the following:

- **Animal sector**

Modern business ideas are strongly related to animals, since the love for dogs and cats mainly, is considered one of the most modern and profitable feelings, for that reason more and more businesses that generate income on a large scale to be oriented to that subject are presented.

There is no doubt that exploiting the affective bond between a master and a pet is a relationship that can be used to create products and services that can increase the quality of life of both, that kind of utility is a great reason why consumers invest.

The best way to create a product or service related to this sector is to visualize any routine activity and ask yourself how

it can be improved or simplified, thus revealing the great opportunity to monetize a series of actions that generate well-being.

The best examples in this area are creating an online pet store, offering dog walking services, pet photography, puppy daycare, rental of accessories for certain animals such as aquariums, pet toys, lost pet searches and healthy food.

Among other pet needs, pet cemetery services, home pet grooming, and occasional counseling to address pet-related issues can be marketed.

- **Ecological sector**

The dynamics of ecology is an obligation today, especially to ensure a better future for future generations, so the way of producing and consuming is being changed drastically, for that reason sustainable processes are gaining a higher level of interest commercially and domestically.

To find a business opportunity within this field, it is essential to observe the environment, to find a disproportionate use of resources, to realize the way in which this type of activity can be improved, as well as to think about designing a second use of some object.

The most popular actions that can be commercialized in this sector are the installation of solar panels, wind installations, proposing models of transport with delivery vehicles or electric means, as well as the creation of green cleaning products without harming the planet, and in the fashion world, ecological lines are being added.

The use of the conservation theme extends to the use of rainwater harvesting, review of the water consumption of a property, and establishment of fruit and vegetable production, along with the use of national components as a way of local entrepreneurship.

- **Antique handicraft sector**

Due to the constant evolution of society and at the same time of the economy, the impact of technology has made different trades are disappearing, one of them is journalism, because this kind of work has been replaced by innovative functions, so you can revive various small activities to spread it with advertising.

The basic idea of paying attention to this sector is to find a niche market where the work of the past can be exhibited, and to focus on that public that prefers the traditional, it is a simple action, but it has a very outstanding potential margin.

In the midst of conventional business opportunities, there is the stone carver, custom shoes, beekeeping action, pipe making, framer, without leaving aside the craft or area of artisanal agriculture, sewing, home hairdressing, and much more that is trending in each geographic location.

- **Real estate sector**

The construction sector has always been in a commercial trend, since it provides the satisfaction of one of the basic needs of each person, for that reason real estate development is an alternative that does not go out of fashion, especially with the option of taking advantage of credits that allow it to be an active sector.

Beyond unfavorable economic situations, real estate continues to grow in the face of every adversity. To be part of this sector, conventional means can be exploited, it is very varied and it is worth studying it in depth, as it is a broad line of business, such as the sale of prefabricated houses, among other measures.

The alternatives that have the greatest probability of success at present are the offer to buy or invest in houses instead of apartments, as well as avoiding the massive purchase of land, since it loses value rapidly, and the exposition of the

advantages of prefabricated houses as one of the most positive themes.

- **Sports sector**

The commercial side of sports is very productive because of the level of passion that inhabits this area, it is a feeling that is above any era, that is why it is an important trend that can be monetized, even to the point of involving the health sector, since the practice of sports is a way to be fit.

Business and sports can go hand in hand, it is a sector that with passion can be taken to a highly lucrative level, you just have to think of profits that can accentuate this type of fanaticism or practice.

Sports promote advantageous business opportunities such as photography of sporting events, installation of recreational centers such as paintball, maintenance of golf courses, sale and exhibition of sporting goods, training academy of any discipline, even opening an adventure sports agency.

The close relationship between entertainment and sports, from offering karting services, to covering the trend of personal coaching, active sports betting media, nutrition articles for

athletes and assistance in creating meal plans, is an area with many creative opportunities.

- **Sector for the elderly**

The population of elderly people is very large all over the world, this scenario demands products or services that imply an improvement in the quality of life, as well as that can be a stimulus for the well-being of their health as the years go by, it is a phenomenon that generates a great number of needs.

Faced with a large percentage of seniors, a variety of business ideas can be implemented with an inclination for the future, or at the same time can impart comfort so that in the future, seniors can enjoy their mature stage.

The assistance that has the greatest commercial potential starts with personalized financial advice for a more peaceful old age, creating a dating web portal for seniors, yoga classes, computer advice for them to make full use of every function, nutrition service and home help for any physical work.

In addition to this, offering health insurance, adjusting homes to facilitate the mobility of the elderly, and other types of support that generate a positive change in the lives of the elderly, is a sector that promotes a high level of investment.

- **Fashion industry**

The clothing and clothing fashion, represent interesting areas through which you can invest, beyond the level of competitiveness that is part of this activity, there is a great opportunity to draw attention, as long as you can bet on innovation, it is a sector in which you can study the trends present.

Find a differential way through which you can take advantage of fashion utilities to sell, you only need to implement effective strategies that allow you to form a scalable business in every way.

One way to exploit this sector with great potential to generate income, is under the sale of second-hand clothing, clothing repair, and in the online world you can set up a blog about fashion, online sale of handmade clothing, on the other hand is the personal image consulting.

As if that were not enough, in the fashion sector you can opt for a much more specialized route, such as the sale of equipment for athletes, sleepwear, and even some kind of attire that is collectible, and there is also the extravagant field, where you can expose the sale of clothing for Barbie dolls.

- **Automotive sector**

The number of vehicle sales has not decreased, over time it is a sector with a large productivity margin, therefore any tool or service has a utility that can be marketed, this facilitates the establishment of a business, so that more people value this type of offering.

The innovative ideas to be implemented in this area start with the purchase and sale of used cars, car sharing services, car parking space sharing, specialization in car tuning, car rental, gasoline payment assistance and even a car repair shop comparator.

- **Restaurant sector**

The world of restaurants is also an area crowded by competition, but it allows to stand out when a clear personality is imposed that can be translated into a flow of sales, by presenting an original idea or theme, with modern food plans, it generates that kind of expected commercial success.

Beyond presenting a modern food proposal, it is a sector that must be willing to innovate and be in constant research to implement the opportunities of the commercial environment.

To jump-start opportunities in the food medium, you can run a business that provides flavors of a particular country

through subscription, catering services tailored to modern trends, snacks in musical boxes or for other purposes, pay for the amount or portion of food someone can eat.

On the other hand, a business can be created for a reduced niche that requires attention, such as the establishment for allergy sufferers, thus providing services for specialized groups.

Through these options provided by each sector, you can create an attractive business, all part of the use of the most prevalent needs, having these aspects in mind you can develop a vision to execute these examples on your location to achieve the expected success.

Innovations and services with a high profit margin

The search for opportunities in any business environment is a constant desire today, with a great passion you can materialize each of the ideas that are having success or demand in each sector, because instead of passing up that energy to undertake, it is time to get going with these alternatives.

Starting a business is easier than it was before, even from scratch with a lot of effort, or with the right investment, you

can scale in the commercial environment, enjoying the advantages of being able to do it even from the comfort of your home, all thanks to the opportunities provided by the internet and your skills.

1. Chatbots Design

The realization of Chatbots, possesses a great relevance today, because every website seeks to improve the treatment or customer service every time, it is an application that uses artificial intelligence for the digital environment to promote assistance, this invention is a great source of job opportunities and is done through programming.

Every company is requesting the creation of Chatbots, the interaction with the customer can be guaranteed by this way, it is even an obligation within the marketing, for that reason, to start programming a Chatbot, you can bet on the free tool of chattypeople.com.

What is needed for the creation of Chatbots, is to learn every detail about the bots and the type of functions to incorporate, then you can create an account in tools such as the above mentioned, to perfect skills, and receive a request, where you must know the expectations of the company to create and launch it.

2. **Accounting services or assistance**

When you have a great passion for numbers, you can take advantage of these skills to monetize them, it is basically to perform as a freelance accountant, although this requires training in this field, and not stop innovating with digital tools that facilitate billing and tax management.

3. **Virtual assistant or personal assistant**

This kind of services may not be very attractive, but over time they have become a function on which a great remuneration is invested, it is useful or ideal for those who are used to have contact with managements over an office, only that it is based on a much more digital version, which generates freedom in both senses.

Currently, different platforms can be used to develop this kind of position, one of the most popular is upwork.com, which allows you to find clients, and enables flexible schedule design options, as well as the type of fee to be established.

4. **Marketing Services**

The application of marketing is known as one of the obligations of modern business, so every work related to this world

is in high demand, but to provide results in this medium, it is essential to have experience and knowledge, this implies that you must invest in training courses.

If you have the necessary tools to offer support on the marketing world, you have a great opportunity to establish a marketing agency, this sector has a great growth curve, it is an area with many forms of specialization or execution, you can even apply as an influencer marketing.

Most modern businesses are in a constant search for freelancers related to marketing, where the text that is transmitted on Google is optimized, and a large series of actions that are aimed at converting visitors into customers, not to mention that the creation and publication of content is in demand.

SEO improvement provides a great opportunity to work, especially to carry out actions such as meta descriptions, appropriate titles, keyword density, tags and categories, to the choice of optimized images that are related to the theme.

5. Social media consulting

The use and charm of social networks is a reality, so when you are an expert in one or your own personal account stands out, you can count on professional training so that you can

do the same with the accounts of others, and that kind of certification is useful to convince large companies.

Today, social media can be classified as an unlimited business, in addition to having an extensive customer base, which means that it is an important source of income, and it is a trend that continues to grow, especially with the emergence of new platforms.

In addition to the possibilities provided by social networks, there are a wide variety of tools that facilitate the management and administration of the same, for this reason it is an environment with many alternatives to meet the objectives set.

6. **Affiliate Marketing**

A very popular method to generate income is affiliate marketing, where the reality of obtaining commissions in exchange for the promotion of products or services of any company is presented, it all consists of choosing a product or service with which you have an affinity or understand completely, to promote it and earn a percentage for each sale.

The sales made through your digital presence, is a simple business that only needs a blog or digital media with audience, demonstration of that amount of audience, and start doing digital marketing, where you should advertise with the results obtained, to perform this action with more companies.

7. **Review writer**

The generation of sales, or propagation of the desire to buy, has led companies to invest in reviews, as it is a confirmation of the quality of services or product, to practice this work, you can create a profile as a freelancer to create this approach with companies, to offer reviews.

To gain conviction about this work, you can create a digital space that proves your writing skills, thereby setting rates based on your talent, based on the construction of a portfolio as a great presentation to receive hires on this activity.

8. **Organizational services**

The organization is a service very similar to that of virtual assistants, it is based on having a remote secretary, for this it is necessary to have communication skills, time management, and a great development of autonomy, causing that the

agenda of appointments, calendar organization, answering emails and much more is fulfilled with excellence.

9. Digital Appointment Query

The ability to communicate, can be exploited to the maximum to relate love topics, that is, the explanation of how to find love, is very profitable, since that can work as a great help for users, this is known as a dating consultant, although it can be interpreted as simple, it is a great responsibility.

Guiding people to find the love of their lives can be a great challenge, although the daily tasks to be performed are managing a profile that classifies you as an expert in this mission, as well as being part of dating apps, writing profiles, and offering matchmaking advice with other people, all require empathy.

10. eBay Seller

It is based on a similar dedication to affiliate marketing, but instead of promoting a product or service, it is basically about dealing directly with the customer, charging a commission to the owner of that product or service at the end of the sale, although this generates many risks by running into fake sellers.

It is important to assume that in this type of sales, the person responsible to the customer is the entrepreneur, so when you are looking for this activity to be profitable, you just have to know the distributor completely, keep the money in the wallet until the satisfactory delivery of the product or service, in addition to giving notice of any suspicious activity.

11. Application development

Every day there is an application of great utility, so developing capabilities to create an application is highly profitable, especially when you have an original idea about any need of users, for that reason you just have to put that desire into action, especially because it does not require a large investment.

To carry out the creation of an application, you can try free developers, tutorials, and also courses, and then apply a good marketing strategy that can publicize the application, so you can generate income, it is a great business that can be developed remotely.

12. Web development

In a world dominated by digitalization, all businesses are obliged to have a website, and in addition to all manage a large

volume of traffic, especially to boost sales of that business sector, so that capacity is useful and profitable, even for companies because they manage to have a digital environment.

The best start to excel in the web development activity is to use Wordpress to build a website, until you can increase your programming skills. To do this you should learn programming language, and use codeacademy.com to the maximum, to learn every detail of a commercially useful website.

13. Cybersecurity review

The constant use of digital media, imposes to be careful about every operation, especially to avoid episodes of hacking, information theft, and all kinds of viruses, thus minimizing threats with increased digital security, this management helps to generate income to take care of digital integrity, for businesses and individuals.

14. Graphic design

The appearance of a business is highly important, this indicates that the realization of designs becomes a profitable talent, because every business seeks to become an unforgettable brand, and to reach that level it was necessary to create an essential footprint, it is necessary to master Photoshop or

Illustrator, to create logos, advertising, newsletters, letters and so on.

15. Publisher

The graphic publication is very useful to broadcast information, therefore these services are quoted to create magazines, books, advertising newsletters and other material pertaining to marketing, it is based on a complete action to make the content impactful and can even create an eye-catching digital product with this work.

16. Business plan design

Business ideas and the desire to emerge abound today, but the organization to make this a reality makes sense, because the development of a business plan helps to win some investor, for that reason if you have training in business management or links with marketing, you can carry out the evaluation of projects.

The functions of this media are based on the creation of authentic texts, so that they can be personalized based on the business, for which different templates can be used and issued to the clients, causing the business to have an in-depth study of its viability.

Each of these ideas are highly innovative, because they address the modern needs that are so sought after, for that reason they mean a wide business opportunity to reap significant profits, you just need vision and ambition, looking for a function that matches your skills.

The most viable businesses in times of crisis

Depending on each era, some types of business are more likely to succeed than others, since crises actually have a lot to do with changing needs, being a point or aspect that can be exploited to generate profits, there are many examples that you can take into account to inspire you.

By studying different sectors with great utility even in times of crisis, you can be part of this global context, taking advantage of the possibilities of these alternatives, each choice is a paradigm and does not work for everyone, but knowing the following businesses, you can compare them with the consumption habits to perform the most interesting.

- **Renting or leasing**

Renting is an option for the public that does not have access to the purchase of cars, clothes and even machinery, is an

approach to the latent needs in times of crisis, because consumers seek to spend less today, for that reason the renting has a wide potential for it is an effective business model.

- **Repair services and repairs**

In the midst of a crisis, the last thing users think about is buying clothes, new appliances, or any other item, for that reason they seek to achieve a second or third utility by carrying out repairs and repairs, being a special business that fits perfectly with a context of economic complication.

- **Recycling and reuse environment**

A sector of the future is the one related to ecology, therefore the commitment to recycling and reuse is a solution to take into account, because in the midst of a recycling is also a profitable measure, the advice of changes in the home or cheaper products for being second human or reused is in great demand.

As you can recycle a product, you extend the possibilities of purchase, it is a great business idea can be adjusted to the passions you possess, they are successful business models because these services are sought after even by lovers of the green trend.

- **Sports**

Beyond any bad economic moment, many social groups are concerned about the practice of sports, either for health or aesthetic issues, for that reason a gym, advice on the medium or sales of articles, is of great relevance, it is not a business alternative that can go out of fashion, but that generates resources frequently.

- **Health care**

There is no doubt that in the midst of a crisis of all kinds, what is most valued is health, and at the same time is the most damaged by the level of stress that this kind of situation causes, this points to a massive demand for psychological assistance, as well as alternative practices to help reduce this damage, such as yoga, meditation and others.

- **The world of cosmetics**

The manifestation of recession generates that the lack of purchase of expensive clothes is substituted by the purchase of makeup, which is one of the safe bets, so above any eventuality, the flow of sales is not affected in a drastic way as it is imagined.

- **Financial assistance**

In the midst of financial problems, it is vital to have financial services, it is now essential to have quick loans, as well as a way to renegotiate debts, so the increase of this type of services in the midst of crisis, makes sense.

- **Legal Specialty**

In any incidence, legal assistance is needed, especially in an environment where bankruptcies occur every day, as well as foreclosure episodes and even foreclosures, so it is an alternative to exploit in the midst of this kind of circumstances.

- **Insurance services**

An investment that is not overlooked in the face of complications is related to insurance, because in the first place is placed the personal care and even on the goods, without leaving aside that it is part of the civil liability, so it is a long-term policy that should not be left unpaid.

- **Crowdfunding and fintech**

In view of the fact that internet connection has become a normality nowadays, offering crowdfunding is a latent need, as

it is the access to obtain a sum of money that can be asked for, it is a viable alternative in the face of difficulties.

- **Management sharing**

Social needs can always be exploited, for that reason offering a collaborative economy is a great opportunity, especially with the establishment of platforms for apartment rentals, car sharing, meals and much more, this can be built through Uber or Airbnb.

- **Coworking**

When there is a clear desire to save money, coworking spaces are a great measure, because in the face of the crisis, it is possible to avoid devaluation, it is a networking action that will later gain value for this type of format.

- **Online stores**

E-commerce can be implemented as a cost saving solution, because this purchasing model is much cheaper, and you have direct access to a large population of users, making it an ideal positioning to generate revenue.

In the midst of the chaos, in the economic world there are ample alternatives to carry out an undertaking that contributes in both directions, since the commercial dynamics is about a contribution for the buyer as well as the seller, and by adjusting to social conditions, this probability of success becomes a reality.

The reasons why crises are good for business start-ups

Market needs are accentuated in the midst of crises, which is why it is a great environment for entrepreneurship. Throughout history, the great companies that are known today originated by taking advantage of times of crisis, as happened with McDonald's, a business idea that grew in large proportions.

The birth of businesses in the face of complexities is part of that necessary character to undertake, being something typical of the economies of the world, since without prior notice negative circumstances may arise such as pandemics, before the new business ideas, only a good foundation is needed to scale commercially.

Great experts in the economic sector, such as Warren Buffett, point out that when the tide goes out in a market, that is

when you can see who is swimming naked at a commercial level, because that is the scenario that manifests itself in a crisis, and mostly businesses that do not have good management, together with high debt, decline.

For this reason, the best projection for a business to be afloat is to innovate, the density of technology is an important solution for each management to be up to date, in addition to adding tools, you can invest in sectors that have or are in constant trend, taking into account the study of financing and the feasibility of each business idea.

How to undertake in the face of difficulties

In the face of dreams to get ahead, personal aspirations can be overshadowed by difficulties such as lack of investment, lack of motivation for economic reasons, or any other reason, for that reason it is only necessary to know in depth the businesses that are booming.

To find this great business opportunity, it is also a great requirement to study the consumer, since under the understanding of their consumption habits can be created and exploit an opportunity for commercial progress to expand, since these are sustainable businesses over time and leave high income rates.

1. Establishing a business dedicated to technology and innovation

Following the trend of attachment to digitalization, any idea related to innovation and technology can be safely exploited, it is a large-scale business model, especially when it is directed on the internet, mobile applications and others, in this sense video editing makes more sense.

Starting a business dedicated to technology is a simple and reliable idea, especially for those who are looking to develop business functions in the digital environment, since you can carry out the execution of an online store, as well as the sale of technology items is listed as a full need.

The more ideas you can have, in relation to technology, the greater the probability of success, to have clarity, you can read magazines on technology trends, review websites or technology businesses implemented in advanced countries, as well as track the best-selling technology product.

2. Franchise opening

In the world, the establishment of franchises has an interesting margin of success, so it is an option with great utility, it is important because a franchise causes that you do not have

to know or be an expert about the management of a company, much less take time looking for a profitable idea.

To be part of a franchise, it is important to consider that group of experts who study the potential of each current business idea, so you can choose one that identifies with your passion, that way you can have access to the use of it, it is simple and fast, one of the most demanded is the "low cost" hospitality and perfumes, this can be adapted to your city.

3. **Offer of products or services dedicated to the luxury sector.**

One of the sectors that is less affected by crisis or complexities is the luxury sector, since in theory it is a commercial offering aimed at a social group with purchasing power, they do not have economic problems, and therefore are active consumers, so it is a safe bet, it can be luxury tourism, luxury products and much more.

When analyzing in depth the social networks of celebrities, you can find many examples of luxury offerings, even taking into account their attire is profitable, because they are profitable ideas that have their own marketing when seen or viralized by celebrities.

4. Alcohol and similar vices

There is no doubt that a consumer sector that remains active above all is tobacco, sex, gambling, among others, for this reason it is a category of business with high demand, regardless of the situation of the locality, so also the nightclubs maintain a high concurrence.

5. Acquisition of a company

In times of crisis, instead of a real estate bet, the most common is to take advantage of the purchase of a company, this can be by means of participations or in its entirety, although this is a business opportunity that requires a high investment, therefore it is not available to everyone.

However, for those who have this in mind, they should think about taking advantage of these offers, since after overcoming some economic difficulty, a possibility of relaunching arises, for which the company must be evaluated beforehand, it is a complete dedication of time and money.

The optimization of a bankrupt business is a feasible bet, although it may also represent a net interest in acquiring that customer base for a different business idea, this opens a wide range of opportunities, especially when a large margin

of knowledge is implemented to make the appropriate decisions.

6. Online business training

The opportunity presented by the online market is resounding, so for large and small entrepreneurs there are options, it is an environment that has no limits and can be exploited in many directions, even in times of crisis the online medium is capable of generating large revenues.

The demand for online shopping is a modern activity, for that reason, being part of this dynamic is a privilege itself, it can also be combined with a physical development, it is a double opportunity.

7. Services and products for sports and health

The realization of therapies is an activity that has no ceiling, even in the face of economic complications, because people seek to free themselves from so many problems, without forgetting that part of the trend is to be part of sports actions, since it is also used as a step to have access to self-improvement.

Personal goals related to sports are increasing every day, so this passion can be exploited with the marketing of products and services related to this growing practice.

8. Consulting for personal and commercial brands

A company or business is kept under a constant desire for renewal, for that reason they opt for services to consolidate a brand, this offering can be provided through training, as well as passion for new emerging technologies, so that companies can be advised to take that step.

This is a job solution with great opportunities, especially if you have skills in programming, database management, positioning, digital marketing, even as a community manager, this kind of areas are in demand by companies, with training in this area, there are plenty of opportunities.

9. Marketing of raw materials and commodities

There is no doubt that the commercial sector that takes care of basic needs, has a high margin of demand, since regardless of the economic situation it is an essential purchase, so

it is a sector to which you can bet especially when it has to do with food, medicine, or any raw material in this sector.

10. Sale of low-cost products

A useful expansion is to be part of the companies that work in the low cost field, this category represents a very broad sector, because the society demands economic products especially in crisis, therefore it is a profitable opportunity where the commercial objective is to generate income under a high volume of sales.

Each one of these 10 developments are a path of entrepreneurship, especially when there are great difficulties and economic obstacles, since they are the commercialization of needs that have a huge boom today, for that reason each one of these alternatives can not be overlooked.

Business opportunities to take advantage of during the crisis

A period of crisis can cause fear in many economic sectors, but in reality it is a great time to apply for a venture, this is due to the decrease of competitors that exist or concur in the market, thus representing a risk that is worth considering, to think about setting up a business.

The opportunity to start a business becomes much more feasible in times of turmoil, in every commercial context, a gap opens up that can be exploited to generate income, it is an option not to overlook, especially when it comes to establishing services for the management of defaults, or opportunities to obtain resources.

Likewise, the labor area has become a popular area for hiring lawyers in view of the large number of layoffs, for this reason, these issues have a large proportion of boom, without forgetting that the consumer sector is an area that has a margin of positive sustainability.

On the other hand, discount stores are becoming a focal point for consumers, as well as food distribution services, and in addition to this, services or items for pets, there is a high margin of opportunities dedicated to the assistance itself, in this point the health sector stands out.

Another highly potential topic is environmental care, especially with the commercialization of renewable energies, biotechnology, as well as the Internet, which are essential elements for society, even online advertising services are a great solution.

Meanwhile, in terms of technological impact, the importance of e-commerce is not lost sight of, where mobile applications are managed so that entrepreneurs can carry out their commercial responsibilities from the device, being an environment in full growth.

However, one of the markets with greater scalability over time is the luxury sector, since it is not affected by any type of commercial decline, but is sustained by the large flow of sales that it generates, these are gaps that should be exploited to the maximum, to stop thinking about postponing the start of a business.

Types of business to be established in the consumer sector

When the economy presents an unstable behavior, the aforementioned opportunity of the lean cows to generate income is presented, although there may be great doubts at the moment of deciding on some type of business, in order not to let this changing panorama prevent you from undertaking, it is vital to know the consumer market.

- **The alcohol business**

Businesses based on alcohol tend to withstand any kind of economic complication, although the type of liquor that is expensive is the one that is recent in this kind of times, therefore the economic liquor has a greater potential to spread it, since the habit of consuming alcohol does not stop even in a crisis.

The adaptation of vices to the crisis is a position of the consumers that can be completely commercialized, therefore a liquor store as well as a distribution of the same, imposes itself as an obvious solution.

- **The cosmetics business**

The beauty industry represents a space that remains alive beyond complications, it is the same impulse as with alcohol, consumers seek in any way to fulfill their aesthetic pretensions, it is also a way to cheer up in the face of adversity.

In view of these reasons, the cosmetics area is vulnerable to recessions, and the ways to be part of this commercial dynamic is through the distribution of catalogs, as well as by setting up an online store.

- **The movie business**

The enjoyment of movies corresponds to an ideal distraction to escape from difficulties, so being part of the promotion of premieres is a way in which you can form a business, although you must be careful with the issue of rights, what you can take advantage of is resale of movie tickets trends, ideal for small locations.

- **The business of health care**

The health sector is very complex to penetrate because of the requirements it has, but it is a growing market, so any fresh idea to revolutionize the distribution of medicines or supplies, what must exist is an attachment to the health conditions that exist on this local sector.

- **The specialty food store business**

Food trends are highly profitable, for that reason any marketing point can be widely exploited, it is a wide popularity to be part of this kind of market of great need, to impact this opportunity you can create a line of products, which highlights the vegan trend or home delivery.

- **The candy and dessert business**

A taste that is not abandoned over some difficulty, is that of desserts, since the consumption of sugar is even a measure of necessity for many people, especially as a way to release stress, the means of consumption is used to leave aside the tensions generated by some discouraging economic environment.

- **The funeral business**

Funeral services are classified as a latent need, so more and more users take care of this aspect to have covered this kind of procedures, these services are not at all pleasant, but they are still highly influential.

- **The tax services business**

In difficult economic times, is when the intervention of an accountant is most needed, to seek to preserve a viable solution to the responsibility with the Treasury, causing that the taxes can be in order, therefore are conditions to be covered with professional advice in the tax area.

This type of consumer market reveals the large number of needs for which the population is willing to pay or afford, for that reason they remain at the top of the business, to cover a large number of years with commercial strength, this can be

taken as a reference to choose those sectors of constant demand.

Businesses capable of surviving a pandemic

Little imaginable in the commercial sector was designing a business that would be able to withstand a pandemic, until the arrival of the coronavirus challenged all kinds of commercial planning, causing investment attractiveness to focus squarely on flexible business models that are resilient in the face of external chaos.

The solution at first sight, has been carried out by the electronic commerce, being the best measure to combat any remoteness with the market, this demands to have a high training to be profiled on this type of commercial interaction, in that way the impact of the pandemic or unforeseen events can be mitigated.

Any kind of business, small or large, with the arrival of a pandemic, its entire way of operating is put to the test, so online sales show a shocking rise of 150% growth, being a scenario that makes anyone rethink the way to run and bet on a business.

To measure the potential of a business model in the face of a pandemic, it is essential that you know the sectors most

likely to overcome this kind of adversity, where four key steps of the modern economy have been set, firstly the concentration of production, local suppliers, technology and finally cooperation.

In the history of financial crises, the hangovers left by the coronavirus are profound, even beyond World War II, especially with the parameters of life that have been established, such as health risks, labor management problems due to telecommuting, and the paralysis of commercial mobility.

That kind of scenario, generates a solid scenario where the percentage of urban deliveries has grown, because e-commerce depends on it, and it is an overtaking that is having over traditional commerce, and deliveries have been a method of innovation for many businesses to stay alive.

- **Business organization today**

This desire to establish a strong business also requires the design of a flexible business model that can adapt to social demands such as a pandemic, and must be ideal for carrying out the duties of both the business manager and the employees.

The market itself imposes conditions to which it is only appropriate to adapt, therefore the current organization begins by creating facilities that allow to comply with the development of modern protocols, that type of presentation is a security for employees, and imparts confidence on customers.

As for the objectives that can be traced, it is vital to be able to set short-term goals, until they are modified in view of modern expectations, causing to be able to respond to every need, to take these steps it is also necessary to meet and measure the needs of users.

The opportunities that arise in a market cannot be overlooked, they are considerations to be able to cover the user experience, although to these changes are also added those of the supply chain, as it has to do with border restrictions, this causes the network of producers to change towards a local direction.

The security in the face of commercial turmoil, is to look for an optimal alternative so that you have the option to extend the choice or options of suppliers, and in the middle of this process you must avoid increasing costs, since in the long term what you care about is profitability, thus maintaining sales in a positive direction.

- **The importance of logistics management**

Supplier networks are the first to be affected by problems such as a pandemic, so the logistics activity must be taken into account, otherwise businesses begin to decline, where it has been shown that there is greater resistance to retail supply chains.

This causes it to be a requirement to have a commercial ally that is in charge of deliveries, this is key for today's businesses, for that reason online stores are able to survive, so it is not a choice to assume lightly, but must comply with all a previous estimate.

- **Technology is a weapon of great potential**

The relevance of mastering the aspects of e-commerce, is a great advantage to develop teleworking with a high margin of productivity, are based on two essential ways for a business to function fully, even the figures support the success of Internet sales and these have a large increase.

As technology becomes much more incorporated into business management, even the mode of operation becomes easier, as you can bet on video call services to shorten times for example, which is a sign that interruptions have no value with the modernity of digitization.

- **Setting up an online store**

Businesses of different sizes have valued the importance of having virtual stores, it is one of the most feasible structures to survive in the face of difficulties, only 30% in the world had a virtual store, but today that figure has increased significantly.

The bet on digital media also entails a necessary investment on marketing agencies, especially to reach a large margin of customers on a global scale, it is a channel that has more favoritism for the acquisition of products to become a reality in a simple way.

However, nowadays, it is not only necessary to set up a web store, but it must be complemented with a first class logistics and storage system, so that the product delivery can be carried out, and it is also necessary to improve active communication with customers to solve their concerns or requirements.

Loyalty on virtual stores depends directly on the previous management carried out, and in a crisis environment, it is essential to maintain active communication with customers, without forgetting the incorporation of teams that help to support an effective customer service to satisfy any need.

- **Telework and cybersecurity**

Facing a time with physical complications, the alternative of working at home is a reality, being a much more profitable action, instead of falling into infrastructure costs, because everything is reduced and this also implies a better time management, but it is a way of working that must be well executed.

At this point it is essential to take care that no sign of chronic stress is manifested, for this point it is crucial to bet on advice to implement this dynamic, causing the working day to be much more effective, it is a profitable and safe transformation in all aspects.

In the midst of work and digital action, it is crucial to maintain a high level of information security, whether it is the data of workers, such as those of customers, deserve vital coverage, so that no theft or damage occurs, evading the action of hackers, it is a dedication that requires resources.

- **Creativity as a vital ingredient**

The manifestation of a crisis demands ingenuity to overcome the impediments, therefore creativity is crucial to put aside the issues related to communication with the customer, so that in the midst of the problems a differential measure can be presented, since every business lives and is profitable by rethinking its operation.

The production in any environment requires constant monitoring, to which the solution of robots is integrated, so that the attention to customers can be guaranteed, because an agile treatment is remembered, especially in the midst of a calamity, to reach that level it is necessary to establish a social listening system as an innovation.

To find more creative ideas, it is necessary to study social networks every day, to check the needs of each sector, this goes beyond supply and demand, because there are concerns at the time of purchase, so the relationship with customers can not be neglected in any way.

How to exploit the profitable business of selling second-hand goods

The second life of products is a modality or alternative that is frequently exhausted in times of crisis, and a large audience chooses to obtain money by selling them, because most of the market seeks to save money with the purchase of this kind of second life products.

To be part of this dynamic of second-hand products, the following alternatives can be exercised:

1. **Used Apple products**

Given the enormous success of Apple, the desire to have any of these products is something common in the market, so it is a profitable option that can be carried out, being a high quality company and acclaimed worldwide, but their products are not cheap, for that reason there is a wide demand to buy these products used.

2. **Second hand baby products**

A stage as fleeting as the growth of a baby demands an enormous amount of products, but as the child grows, articles such as clothes, crib toys, cars, and any other similar items

become outdated or unusable, even if they are not even used, even with utilities in optimal conditions.

Such items can be useful for other families, so it becomes an effective business for parents, since by buying second-hand items that are in good condition they can save, and even sell them to whoever needs them, this concept is called Baby Eco, where baby clothes are rented.

3. **Second hand furniture**

A large and frequently repeated investment within households is furniture, but a solution through which it is possible to intervene in this environment is through the demand that exists in people who go to reputable stores, where competitive prices are offered, to the point of forming distributors.

4. **Any product with sufficiently high new value**

When you want to be part of the sale of second hand products, you can think of all kinds of products that are manufactured to perform for many years, and above all that has a high value in the market, because that is the way to think or design in a resale, thus selecting a candidate product for resale.

This area of business is interesting, because saving by itself is a trend nowadays, this causes that it is possible to think of a business opportunity through products that have a second utility, that extension of value is useful for the demand that wishes to obtain a product without spending or investing the current market value.

How to finance a business without the help of investors or the bank

A large number of business ventures are left without taking off because of the impediment of financing, but in the face of this problem, alternative means of raising money can be chosen, without having to think about investors, much less banks, it is based on the ability for a resale product to be sold effectively.

The strategy to carry out this kind of entrepreneurship, is under the strategy of closing a contract with a client, to later concentrate on the sale of that modified version of the product, this type of dynamic can be executed by large or small businesses, even Bill Gate used this strategy in its beginnings.

- **Marketplaces**

In the past, the ideal business was based on the installation of a store, but nowadays it has been determined just the opposite, since this is not a requirement or a means to reach customers, instead a medieval practice has been used that has positive results in spite of time, such as the marketplaces.

That is to say in the past it was traded just by a public auction, but nowadays you can pay for the rental of a space in the public square, to gain that space through which these transactions can be materialized, this can be merged with the creation of some platform, to have a physical delivery place.

Having this mode of operation, completely reduces the expenses or the level of investment necessary to emerge, in addition it is not essential to have inventory or any other similar requirement, it is a very low cost that allows to develop the venture to the fullest, other options is to use intermediaries, as part of the collaborative economy.

- **Scarcity model**

The scarcity method, has to do with the promotion of a product, appealing to the exhaustion of the product, it is based on a theory of inciting the customer, it is a really useful tactic, especially in the retail market, this kind of thematic is carried

out in the fashion sector by Zara stores, where it appeals to the passionate public.

- **Subscription model**

It refers to a purchase commitment made by the customer, to deliver that product or service under the agreed term, this is maintained for an extended period of time, it is based on a formula so that customers can be part of the financing of the business itself, this is useful and practiced with electronic products such as magazines.

- **Payment in advance**

It is a way to have access to advances, it is known as a way of financing also, in the first world countries this is a very practiced dynamic, although it is used on consulting services, in that way you reach clients who are in charge of financing you, you must estimate the expenses, so that the clients can pay a part to attend them.

In this way, you can practice this type of payment strategies, which allow you to avoid the necessary budget for physical space issues, as well as to develop a product or service, and you can even guarantee the operation of the business for a

longer time, it is about planning in figures the momentum that requires a business.

How to build an attractive business

The formation of a business idea, demands an economic push, which can be easily achieved when sharing that authentic side behind a business project, it all depends on the level of interest that can awaken, so the prior preparation of a business idea makes more sense.

Reaching that level of attractive presentation is easy when you follow a series of factors that connect in a personal way with your ideals, as well as with the purpose of the business, although before taking any step, it is vital to question the type of business that is suitable for your business idea.

The essential thing is to reflect the potential of that business idea, as well as the planning to make it a reality, which is simple when you practice the following actions that serve as a guide for you to prosper at a commercial level.

1. **Confidence in your idea**

It is essential to demonstrate that this business idea has a high return potential, as this is vital for an investor to be encouraged to take that step forward for your idea, you must

also reflect the type of benefits that you can count on to boost your business, but more than anyone else, the entrepreneur himself is the one who must trust the business idea.

For this reason, the first step to take is to measure the impact of the business idea on the market, this is possible by preparing every detail as if you were going to sell your idea, this type of vision helps to transmit with confidence every aspect of the project, to a level of confidence that is motivating until they believe in your proposal.

2. Analyze the most suitable type of partners

Before thinking about a partner, it is necessary to imagine what kind of skills and qualities he/she should have, as this helps to form a proper business relationship, as this is useful in the long run for a business, because the investor can be a key part of the team of that business idea.

What most investors are looking for is a formal environment to use their money, in addition to being a scalable medium, to think directly about the return on investment on the project, so it is essential to develop each idea with responsibility and seriousness for the investor to connect with these guidelines.

3. Concentration on a single type of investment

In the middle of the management of a business, it is fundamental that the financing comes from the same point, so that it is a reliable source of income, to cover the needs of the project, it must be simplified in figures, until reaching the adequate level, for this reason every future investment must have every movement foreseen.

Planning also incorporates marketing strategies that must be translated into figures, because every minimum detail must be taken into account to arrive at a total cost, and it is also necessary to ensure that the investor receives the lowest possible percentage, it is a mix between realism and what is best for the business, in addition to preventing expenses.

4. An attractive business plan

The preparation of a business plan makes more sense, because it is the presentation and evaluation of the business idea, so that in the business sector the business idea reaches a greater impact, these previous steps determine future problems, thus measuring whether it is a long-term business opportunity.

The objectives within a business plan is a facilitation, because in that way the environment understands the credibility of the business idea, as well as its feasible role, for this reason when making this tool should involve a dynamic, accurate and explanatory vision, to find the ideal partners.

The duties of controlling the finances of a business

The role as an entrepreneur extends to assume more and more functions, these actions drive the obtaining of the first sales to create a sustainable model, to reach that, you can incorporate certain references of the amount of money that has been spent, and income, it happens not to lose the north of the subject.

The control of the financial aspects, is manifested when the clear and attractive aspects of the numbers are recognized, to measure the feasible side of a business with the following steps:

1. Organizational application using Excel

Anyone can think of chaos when you mention Excel, but it is a very valuable tool, so you can design the scale of a product, it is based on a pro design through numbers, this resource is

a great ally in the business world, so to start you can create financial templates that suit your business.

2. Interpretation of numbers to make decisions

Before any step related to the business, the best guidance is the numbers themselves, since they give a great clarity of what each decision implies, and also the type of results that are being generated with the start-up of the business, financial information is a great advisor in all senses.

The first thing to include on this information is the available resources, since this marks a limit itself, allowing each allocation to be consistent with what is allowed, to this is added the estimation of personal finances, because at the beginning all resources are invested, and it is vital to cover making ends meet.

The management of your own resources, helps you to be an expert with the available elements of the company, at the beginning help is required for this point, as well as an issue of invoices to document each step and what it costs to get there, it must be assumed that each choice generates or depends on a cost.

- **Consideration of available resources**

Knowing the availability of resources is a daily action, because it is an indicator of what can be done, it is a business health report, because it is the way to detect each of the financial movements of the business, it is a routine activity with which you must become familiar.

To know if a business can make ends meet or not, as well as fulfill the duties, can be known by having a follow-up of the account, that helps to work on the basis of that punctual amount.

- **The business box**

In the world of treasury, it is a must that the liquidity can be controlled to the point of covering unforeseen events, this type of management helps to create a box to solve various specific problems, it is a creation that is known as a lifeline, without losing focus that the dynamic to follow is to sell, collect and control every expense.

In this way a meticulous management of a business is carried out, because its formation at the beginning requires a lot of effort, but if to that is added a carelessness with the financial part, it will not become profitable as expected, above being

the best business idea, this causes that it is necessary to carry out these steps.

Content

- How to undertake and take advantage of business opportunities 5
- Tips for developing a business opportunity 9
- Software-based productive business trends 12
- What you should know about crowdfunding 19
- Find out how to determine the level of financing for a business 20
- How to finance the commercial launch of a project 22
- Business ideas for each productive sector 28
- Innovations and services with a high profit margin 36
- The most viable businesses in times of crisis 46
- The reasons why crises are good for business start-ups 51
- How to undertake in the face of difficulties 52
- Business opportunities to take advantage of during the crisis 58
- Types of business to be established in the consumer sector 60
- Businesses capable of surviving a pandemic 64
- How to exploit the profitable business of selling second-hand goods 71
- How to finance a business without the help of investors or the bank 73
- How to build an attractive business 76
- The duties of controlling the finances of a business 79

Business opportunities
for times of crisis